NEPTUNE

MARYSA STORM

BLACK
RABBIT
BOOKS

Bolt Jr. is published by Black Rabbit Books
P.O. Box 227, Mankato, Minnesota, 56002.
www.blackrabbitbooks.com
Copyright © 2023 Black Rabbit Books

Michael Sellner, designer and photo researcher

Names: Storm, Marysa, author.
Title: Neptune / by Marysa Storm.
Description: Mankato, Minnesota : Black Rabbit Books, [2023]
Series: Bolt Jr. space explorer | Includes bibliographical
references and index. | Audience: Ages 6-8 | Audience:
Grades K-1 | Summary: "Suit up! Neptune is a planet like
no other, and it's time to explore it through a colorful design
that features vibrant photography, engaging infographics, and
carefully leveled text"– Provided by publisher.
Identifiers: LCCN 2021022213 (print) | LCCN 2021022214
(ebook) | ISBN 9781623107765 (hardcover) |
ISBN 9781644665978 (paperback) |
ISBN 9781623107840 (ebook)
Subjects: LCSH: Neptune (Planet)–Juvenile literature.
Classification: LCC QB691 .S76 2023 (print) | LCC QB691
(ebook) | DDC 523.48–dc23
LC record available at https://lccn.loc.gov/2021022213
LC ebook record available at https://lccn.loc.gov/2021022214

Image Credits

Alamy: dotted zebra, 4-5; Irina Dmitrienko, 6-7; Getty: Erik
Simonsen, 16-17; MARK GARLICK, 4-5; iStock: XtockImages, 18-
19; Science Source: DETLEV VAN RAVENSWAAY, 1, 12-13, 22-23;
John R. Foster, 18-19; MARK GARLICK, 10-11; Walter Myers, 8-9;
Shutterstock: 24K-Production, 10-11; arvitalyaart, Cover; Bikomins,
3, 24; Mopic, 14-15; NASA, 6-7; SkyPics Studio, 20-21; Vadim
Sadovski, 20-21; Vectorfair.com, 14-15; Vector Tradition, 12-13

Contents

Chapter 1
Meet the Planet 4

Chapter 2
Its Place in Space 10

Chapter 3
Explore! 16

More Information 22

Meet the Planet

About 2.8 billion miles (4.5 billion kilometers) from the sun, Neptune spins. The planet is big. It's blue. **Faint** rings surround it.

faint: not clearly seen

COMPARING SIZES

Neptune
96,129 miles
(154,705 km)
around

Huge

Neptune isn't just large. It's cold and icy. People call it an "ice giant." It's nearly four times bigger than Earth.

▶ **Earth**
24,901 miles
(40,074 km)
around

Features

very cold

storms

blue color

faint rings

windy

CHAPTER 2

Its Place in Space

Neptune is an **outer planet**.

It's the farthest from the sun. This distance makes the planet super cold. It's about -330 degrees Fahrenheit (-201 degrees Celsius).

outer planet: any of the solar system's planets that lie beyond the asteroid belt

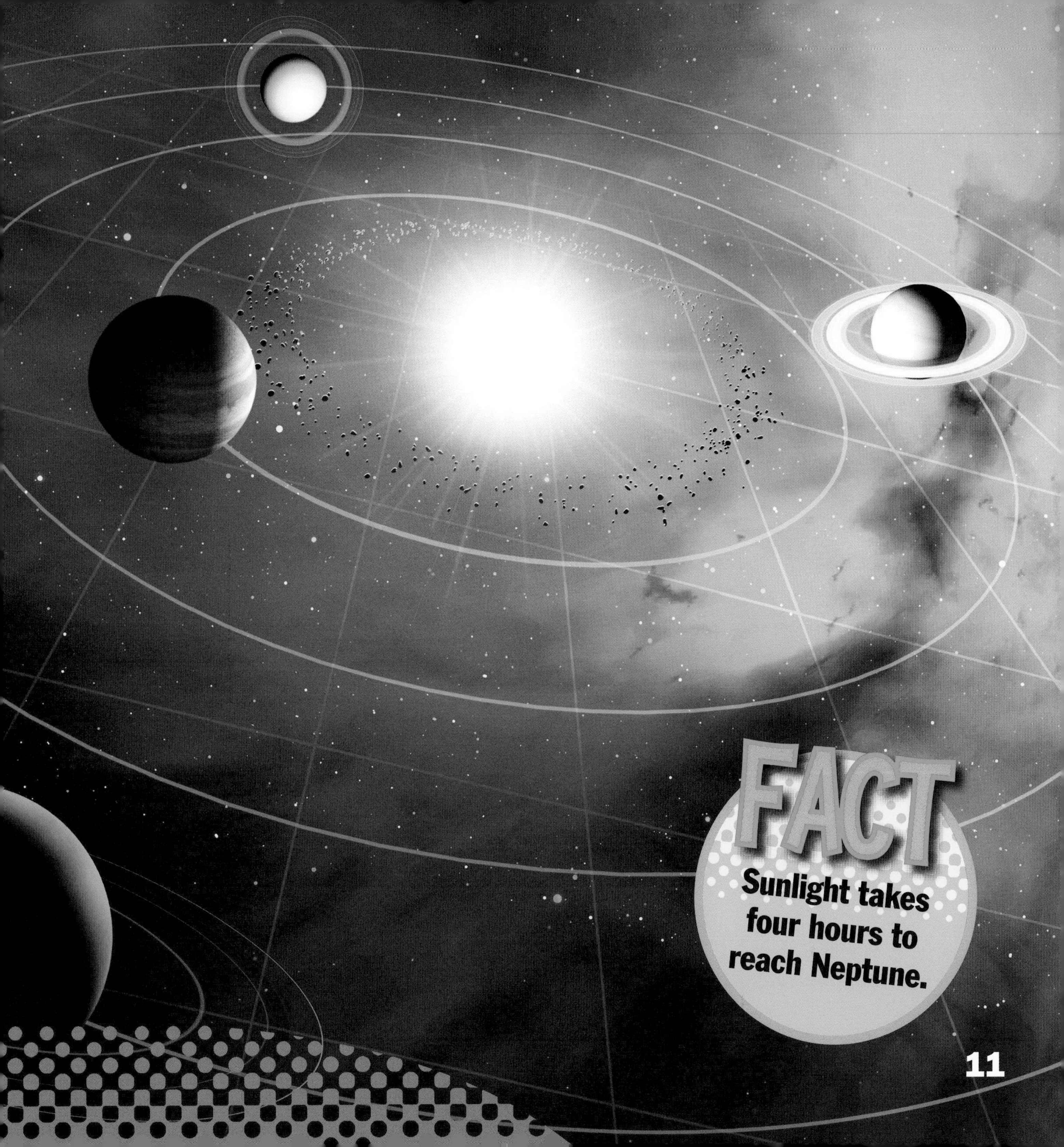

FACT

Sunlight takes four hours to reach Neptune.

Winds

Neptune has superfast winds. They reach more than 1,200 miles (1,931 km) per hour. That's faster than any of Earth's **hurricanes**.

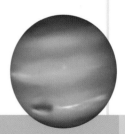

hurricane: an extremely large and powerful storm with very strong winds

Neptune in the Solar System

Mars

Earth

Venus

Mercury

Neptune

Uranus

Saturn

Jupiter

asteroid
belt

CHAPTER 3

Explore!

People don't know much about Neptune. Only one spacecraft has ever visited. It learned about the planet's moons. It studied the rings.

FACT

Voyager 2 reached the planet in 1989.

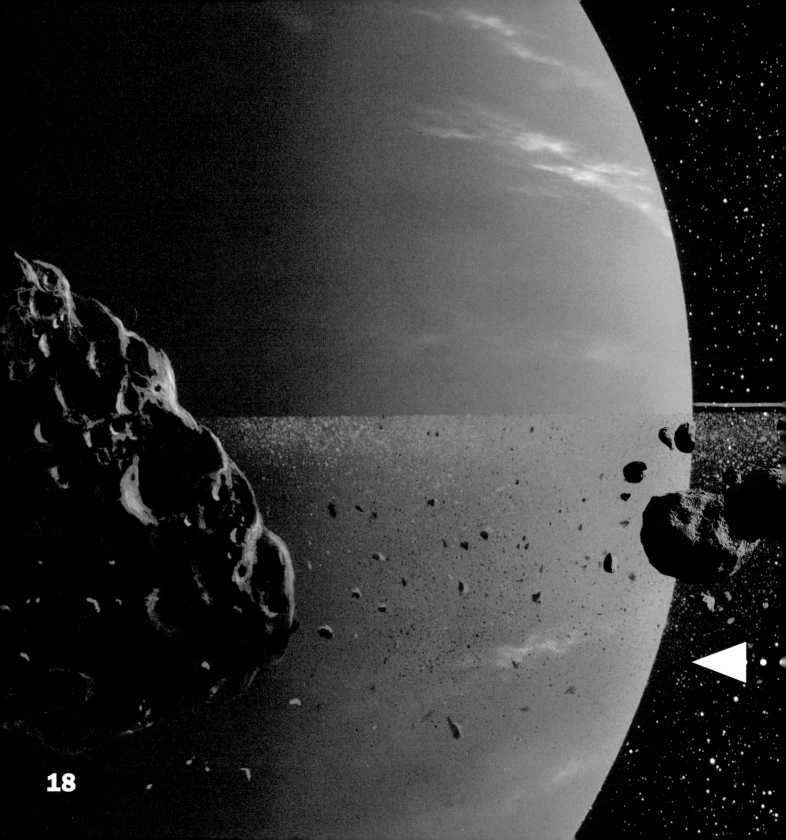

The Future

It takes about 10 years to reach Neptune. And space travel isn't easy. But maybe someday, another craft will make the trip.

············**how far Neptune is from Earth**
about 2.7 billion miles
(4.3 billion km)

Bonus Facts

Neptune has 14 moons.

One day lasts 16 hours.

People don't know what causes the strong winds.

Its core is rocky.

core: the central part of a planet or other body

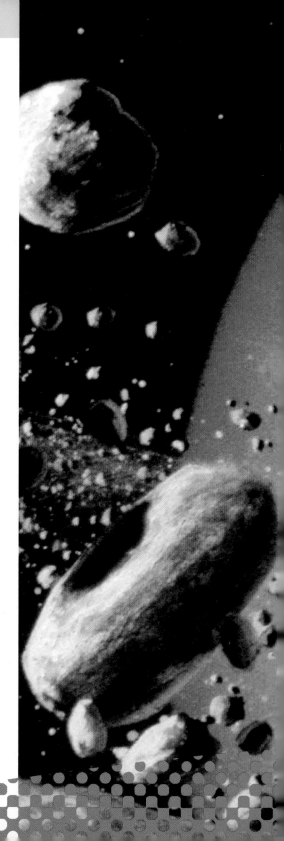

Golusky, Jackie. *Explore Neptune.* Planet Explorer. Minneapolis: Lerner Publications, 2021.

Grack, Rachel. *Curious about Neptune.* Curious About. Mankato, MN: Amicus/ Amicus Ink, 2022.

Loh-Hagan, Virginia. *Space.* Weird Science. Ann Arbor, MI: Cherry Lake Publishing Group, 2022.

All about Neptune
spaceplace.nasa.gov/all-about-neptune/en/

Mission to Neptune
kids.nationalgeographic.com/space/
article/mission-to-neptune

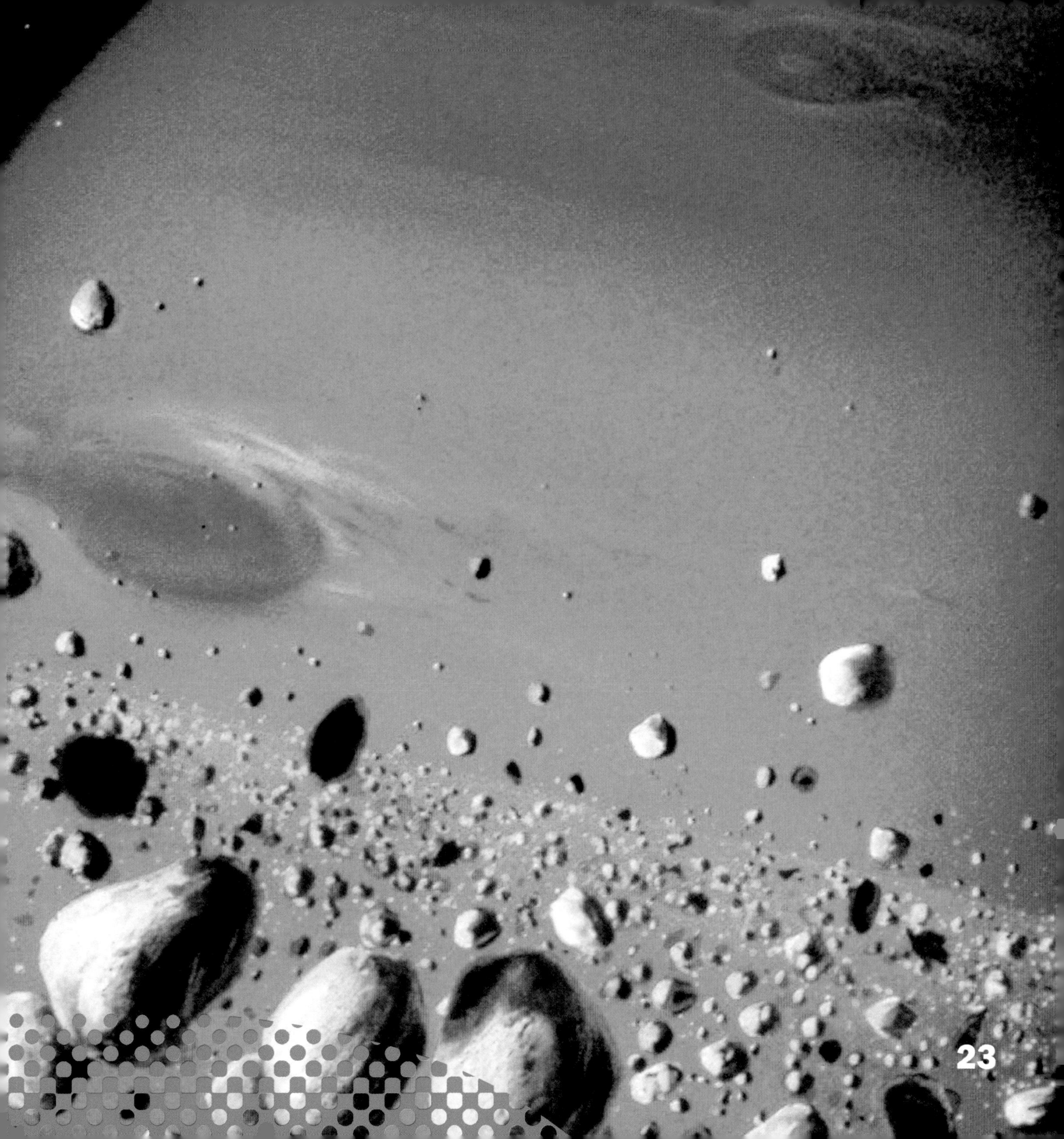

GLOSSARY

core (KOHR)—the central part of a planet or other body

faint (FEYNT)—not clearly seen

hurricane (HUR-i-keyn)—an extremely large and powerful storm with very strong winds

outer planet (OU-ter PLAN-it)—any of the solar system's planets that lie beyond the asteroid belt

INDEX

E
exploration, 16, 19

F
features, 4, 7, 8–9, 13, 16, 21

M
moons, 16, 20

S
sizes, 4, 6–7

T
temperatures, 7, 8, 10

W
winds, 9, 13, 21